CountryMusic ★ Stars
RASCAL FLATTS

By Jeffrey Sooner

Gareth Stevens
Publishing

Please visit our Web site www.garethstevens.com. For a free color catalog of all our high-quality books, call toll free 1-800-542-2595 or fax 1-877-542-2596.

Library of Congress Cataloging-in-Publication Data

Sooner, Jeffrey.
 Rascal Flatts / Jeffrey Sooner.
    p. cm. — (Country music stars)
 Includes index.
 ISBN 978-1-4339-3617-3 (pbk.)
 ISBN 978-1-4339-3618-0 (6-pack)
 ISBN 978-1-4339-3616-6 (library binding)
 1. Rascal Flatts (Musical group)—Juvenile literature. 2. Country musicians—United States—Biography—uvenile literature. I. Title.
 ML3930.R27S66 2010
 782.421642092'2--dc22
 [B]
                                        2009037569

Published in 2010 by Gareth Stevens Publishing
111 East 14th Street, Suite 349
New York, NY 10003

Copyright © 2010 Gareth Stevens Publishing

Designer: Haley Harasymiw
Editor: Mary Ann Hoffman

Photo credits: Cover (background) Shutterstock.com; cover (Rascal Flatts), p. 1 © Jon Kopoloff/FilmMagic; pp. 5, 17 © Rusty Russell/Getty Images; pp. 7, 11, 15 © Jason Merritt/Getty Images; pp. 9, 27 © Andrew H. Walker/Getty Images; pp. 13, 29 © Ethan Miller/Getty Images; p. 19 © Christina Radish/Getty Images; p. 21 © Frazer Harrison/Getty Images; p. 23 © M. Caulfield/WireImage; p. 25 © Kevin Winter/Getty Images.

Printed in the United States of America

CPSIA compliance information: Batch #CW10GS: For further information contact Gareth Stevens, New York, New York at 1-800-542-2595.

CONTENTS

THREE COUNTRY STARS

Rascal Flatts is not a person. It is a band. There are three men in Rascal Flatts.

5

GARY LeVOX

Gary LeVox was born in Columbus, Ohio. He was born in 1970. His real name is Gary Wayne Vernon Jr.

LeVox is Gary's stage name. It means "the voice." Gary is the lead singer for the band.

JAY DeMARCUS

Jay DeMarcus was also born in Columbus, Ohio. He was born in 1971. He is Gary's cousin.

11

Jay plays the guitar and keyboard. He sings and writes music, too.

13

JOE DON ROONEY

Joe Don Rooney was born in a small Kansas town in 1975. He grew up in Oklahoma.

15

Joe Don plays lead guitar. He also sings harmony.

17

GETTING TOGETHER

Gary, Jay, and Joe Don began singing together in 1999. They formed Rascal Flatts in Nashville, Tennessee.

MORE THAN MUSIC STARS!

Rascal Flatts is very well liked. The band works hard. The group often performs to raise money to help people.

HIT SONGS!

Rascal Flatts made its first record in 2000. It was a big hit! The band has had many number one songs.

VOCAL ARTISTS

Rascal Flatts was the top new country vocal group in 2000. The band has won the country Vocal Group of the Year award many times!

25

People love the music of Rascal Flatts.

The band has many fans.

Fans come to hear Rascal Flatts perform. They also come to see the wonderful light show!

TIMELINE

1970   Gary LeVox is born in Ohio.

1971   Jay DeMarcus is born in Ohio.

1975   Joe Don Rooney is born in Kansas.

1999   The band forms and begins singing together.

2000   Rascal Flatts has its first hit record.

2000   Rascal Flatts wins its first Vocal Group of the Year award.

FOR MORE INFORMATION

Books:

Bertholf, Bret. *The Long Gone Lonesome History of
  Country Music*. New York: Little, Brown Books for Young
  Readers, 2007.
Handyside, Christopher. *Country*. Chicago, IL: Heinemann
  Library, 2006.

Web Sites:

Rascal Flatts
www.rascalflatts.com

Rascal Flatts
**hollywoodrecords.go.com/lyricstreet/rascalflatts/
rascalflatts.html**

Up Close with Rascal Flatts Lead Singer Gary LeVox
**www.rd.com/your-america-inspiring-people-and-stories/
up-close-with-rascal-flatts-lead-singer-gary-levox/
article122215.html**

GLOSSARY

award: a prize given for doing something well

cousin: a child of one's uncle or aunt

harmony: pleasing sounds that mix with other sounds

keyboard: a musical instrument with a row of keys like a piano

perform: to sing and play for an audience

stage name: a name used by a musician or actor when he or she is working

vocal: using the voice

INDEX